American Inside Out Evolution

Workbook | Pre-Intermediate | A

SUE KAY
VAUGHAN JONES
PHILIP KERR

macmillan education

Macmillan Education
Companies and representatives throughout the world
American Inside Out Evolution. Workbook Pre-Intermediate A

D.R. © Macmillan Publishers, S.A. de C.V., 2017
Text D.R. © Sue Kay, Vaughan Jones, and Philip Kerr, 2017
Adapted by Peter Maggs and Catherine Smith / The Content Station team: Simon Campbell, George Wells, and Catherine Gray
Macmillan is a registered trademark.
First edition published 2017

ISBN: 978-607-473-637-3

Based on New American Inside Out Workbook Pre-Intermediate A
D.R. © Macmillan Publishers, S.A. de C.V. 2009
Published under license from Macmillan Publishers Ltd.

Editorial Manager: Patricia Muradas
Editorial Operations Coordinator: Veronica Teodorov Ferreira
Editor: Cintia Zaitune
Concept design: Martha Tadaieski
Page make-up: The Content Station
Illustrations: Karen Ahlschläger pp 12, 15, 22, 25
Graphic Production: Kelly Gobbo
Photographic research: The Content Station
Cover concept and design: Jean Aranha
Cover photo: Giovanni Gagliardi | Dreamstime

The authors and publishers would like to thank the following for permission to reproduce their photographs:
Dreamstime / Dmitriy Shironosov p4, Dreamstime / Anastasiya Sytnik p5(t), Dreamstime / Svyatoslav Lypynskyy p6(lt), Dreamstime / Yuliya2206 p6(lb), Dreamstime / Wavebreakmedia Ltd p6(r), Dreamstime / Bflorky p8, Dreamstime / Stbernardstudio p10 (living room), Dreamstime / Guillohmz p10 (bathroom), Dreamstime / Weixin Shen p10 (bedroom), Dreamstime / Sjankauskas p10 (kitchen), Dreamstime / Photomall p10 (dining room), Dreamstime / Severija p11(a), Dreamstime / Сергей Толмачев p13, Dreamstime / Andrei Krauchuk p14(a), p14(c), p14(f), p14(h), Dreamstime / Poemsuk Kinchokawat p14(b), Dreamstime / Ildar Galeev p14(d), Dreamstime / Birgit247 p14(e), Dreamstime / Kakigori p14(g), Dreamstime / Iakov Filimonov p16, Dreamstime / Starserfer p17(a), Dreamstime / Avian p17(b), Dreamstime / Beaniebeagle p17(c), Dreamstime / 1evgeniya1 p17(d), Dreamstime / Oksana Saman p17(e), Dreamstime / Firelia p17(f), Dreamstime / Vadim Vexler p18(a), Dreamstime / Robert Brown p18(b), Dreamstime / Dreamerve p18(d), Dreamstime / Belinka p18(e), Dreamstime / Aldanna p18(r), Dreamstime / Fabio Lotti p22, Dreamstime / Handmademedia p24, Dreamstime / Nefedov Pavel Nikolaevich p25(a), Dreamstime / Maxwell De Araujo Rodrigues p25(b), Dreamstime / Victor Gladkiy p25(c), Dreamstime / Sergiy Rudenko p25(d), Dreamstime / Jara3000 p25(f), Dreamstime / Kostyantin Pankin p25(g), Dreamstime / Alancotton p25(h), Dreamstime / Nerthuz p25(i), Dreamstime / Sidelnikov p27(c), Dreamstime / Lupoalb68 p27(d); **Getty Images** / Neilson Barnard / Staff p5(b), Getty / Jean-Pierre Lescourret p9, Getty / Martin Child p11(b), Getty / Bloomberg / Contributor p11(c), Getty / Dan Dalton p17(l), Getty / Sam Diephuis p18(c), Getty / Han Myung-Gu / Contributor p19, Getty / Sven Hagolani p20, Getty / Merten Snijders p25(tl), Getty / Juanmonino p27(a), Getty / Glow Images, Inc p27(b), Getty / Digital Vision p27(e), Getty / Jupiterimages p27(f)

CANIEM No. 2275

Macmillan Publishers S.A. de C.V.
Insurgentes Sur 1886
Col. Florida, CP 01030
Álvaro Obregón
Ciudad de México
Tel: +52 (55) 5482 2200
elt@grupomacmillan.com

www.grupomacmillan.com www.macmillan.com.mx www.macmillanenglish.com

Printed in Brazil

This book was printed in October, 2018 by: Pancrom Indústria Gráfica, Avenida Engenheiro Billings, 2227/2299
Jaguaré - São Paulo - SP

Contents

1 Name

Grammar

1 **Match the verb tenses in the box with the underlined verbs below.**

future *(be) going to*	~~present perfect~~	
present progressive	simple past	simple present

a Have you ever heard of anyone named "Sky"?
present perfect.

b His parents named him after a painter.

c How do you practice English at home?

d I'm going to work in the games department.

e It's the best sushi I've ever tasted.

f What are you going to do this evening?

g When did you last read a book in English?

h Why are you learning English?

2 **Insert the auxiliary verbs from the box in the sentences below.**

am	are	do
does	~~did~~	did
has	have	is

a His parents^not give him a typical Mexican name. *(did)*
b He never broken the law.
c He not go on vacation last year.
d I going to have coffee after the class.
e I not have my purse with me right now.
f She not want to see me.
g She reading a book about Hawaii.
h They learning English for their work.
i We never been to New York.

3 **Write the sentences in the negative.**

a Dave and I live in the same town.
Dave and I don't live in the same town.

b He knows me very well.

c He can understand my problems.

d He's done very well in his job.

e Our parents were very good friends.

f We went to the same school.

g We're thinking about getting married.

h We're going to have a big party.

4 **In the following sentences, delete *like* when it should not be there. Check (✓) the four correct sentences.**

a He always looks like terrible early in the morning.
b He looks like a very friendly person.
c My ex-husband looked like our dog.
d They looked like tired after the class.
e She looks like a typical middle-aged mother.
f She looks like foreign – is she Brazilian?
g My father-in-law looks like Dracula. Only kidding!
h You look like very stressed. What's wrong?
i The teacher looks like very young.

5 **Write the words in the correct order to make questions.**

a the USA been ever to you Have ?

Have you ever been to the USA?

b are today wearing you What ?

____

c do What kind of read things you ?

____

d your smartphone How do often use you ?

____

e are class in many people there your How ?

____

f an When class did English have last you ?

____

g are English going How many study to years you ?

____

Write true answers to the questions.

6 **Correct the questions with grammatical mistakes. Check (✓) the correct questions.**

a What you are holding in your hand?

What are you holding in your hand?

b What have you eaten today?

____

c Who did you saw last night?

____

d What are you thinking about?

____

e How much money does you have in your pocket?

____

f How many brothers are you have?

____

g How far have you walked today?

____

Write true answers to the questions.

Vocabulary

1 **Read the information and complete the names on John Lennon's family tree.**

a Julian's stepmother is named Yoko.

b Julian's half-brother has a girlfriend named Charlotte.

c One of John Lennon's half-sisters had the same name as his mother.

d Mimi has a niece named Jacqui.

e John had a grandmother named Mary.

John Lennon's family tree, see below.

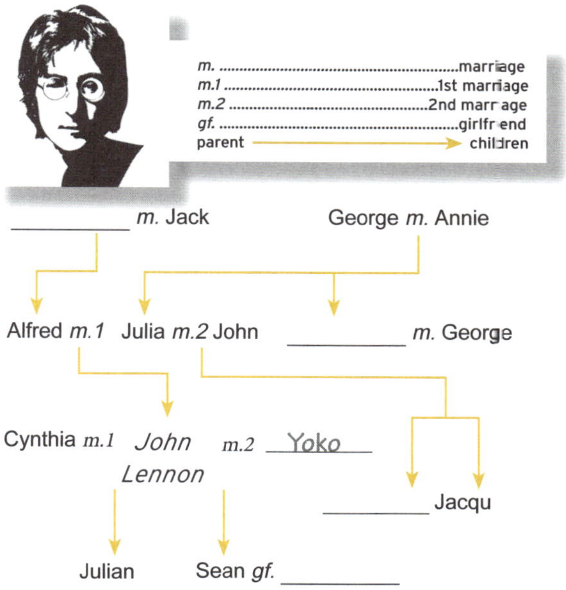

2 **Look at the completed family tree. Are these sentences true (*T*) or false (*F*)?**

a John Lennon's wife was Mimi's nephew *F*

b Alfred's ex-wife was named Julia. _____

c Yoko was Jack's sister-in-law. _____

d Annie was Cynthia's aunt. _____

e Julian was Jacqui's stepson. _____

f John's stepfather was also named John. _____

g George's father-in-law was also named George. _____

h John Lennon had an uncle named Jack. _____

3 **Complete the text with the words in the box.**

~~first~~	husband	initials
last name	maiden	middle
nicknames		

The singer Beyoncé has an unusual name. Beyoncé is her (1) *first* name, and her (2) ________ is Knowles-Carter. Her (3) ________ name, Giselle, is also unusual. Her parents named her after her mother, Tina Knowles. Tina's (4) ________ name was Beyoncé, from her French-speaking family in Louisiana. Beyoncé's (5) ________, B.G., are the same as the rapper B.G. (Baby Gangsta). B.G. has worked with Beyoncé's (6) ________, the rapper Jay-Z. Beyoncé has at least two (7) ________: Bee and JuJu.

4 Put the lines of the text in the correct order.

Jean-François Herremans-Costa Dachelet

a after my grandfather, Jean-François. They also gave me both

b from my father, Paul Herremans. She got married

c I have a problem every time I sign

d is even worse, because she's named Gabrielle-Antoinette.

e my name because it's so long. My parents named me

f their last names, Herremans-Costa. But my mother, Alice Costa, got divorced

g last name, also. My twin sister's signature

h to my stepfather, Michel Dachelet. They added his

1	2	3	4	5	6	7	8
c							d

5 Complete the descriptions of the people with the words in the box.

beard	beautiful smile	blond
eyes	good-looking	~~short~~

My brother David has (1) short,
(2) ______________ hair and green
(3) ______________. He has a
(4) ______________ and a mustache.
I don't think he's very
(5) ______________, but he has a
(6) ______________.

brown	cute	medium-length	straight

My daughter Ruby is very
(7) ____________. She has
(8) ____________, (9) ____________,
brown hair and (10) ______________
eyes.

6 Underline the correct phrase.

Mike: We had a really good weekend.

Wanda: (1) **Oh, no! / Really?** What did you do?

Mike: Well, our new neighbors have a big backyard with a pool.

Wanda: (2) **Does it? / Do they?** Nice!

Mike: Yes, and they had a party for everyone in the neighborhood. All weekend – Saturday and Sunday!

Wanda: Wow! (3) **That sounds great. / That's terrible.**

Mike: Fantastic weather, great food, really friendly people. We danced for hours.

Wanda: (4) **Great! / I know.**

Mike: And Tom Clyde, the new neighbor – he's a TV star.

Wanda: Tom Clyde? (5) **How about you? / I've never heard of him.**

Mike: Yes, you have. He does the Arts Show on Monday nights.

Wanda: Oh, him! (6) **Unfortunately! / Wow!** Can you invite me next time?

02 **Listen and check.**

Pronunciation

1 03 **Listen to the pronunciation of the /ə/ sound in the underlined words.**

A: What did you do over the weekend?

B: Nothing special. How about you?

A: We went for dinner with the neighbors. We went to "The Plaka" – a new Greek restaurant.

B: What was it like? I've never been there.

A: Great. And the waiters were great, too.

Listen again and repeat.

2 Underline the /ə/ sounds in the sentences below.

a What's the word order for negatives?

b I'm going to have coffee after the class.

c Write new vocabulary on a piece of paper.

d My brother is going to be a banker.

04 **Listen and check. Repeat the sentences**

Writing

Filling in a form with personal information.

1 Fill in the registration form for a social networking service.

InsideOutRevolutionNetwork/membership

"Online Insideouters is a great new social networking service which puts you in touch with other English language students around the world."

Complete the registration form and join us now!

Title:

First name:

Last name:

Nickname (optional):

Street address:

Town / City:

Zip / Postal code:

Date of birth: MONTH: DAY: YEAR:

Occupation: *(if you are a student, please say which subjects you study)*

Interests:

How often do you go online?

Reasons for learning English:

Write about yourself and your family:

Sign Up

2 The World

Grammar

1 **Underline the countable noun in each group of words.**

a air-conditioning architecture castle excitement
b advice destination money transportation
c bridge food music weather
d furniture vacation news work
e homework love nightlife office
f knowledge scenery tooth traffic

2 **Complete the text with *so* or *such*.**

Florida is (1) __such__ a great place to go on vacation in the winter. The weather's (2) ______ warm! You can wear just shorts and a T-shirt, and the beaches are (3) ______ quiet. We found (4) ______ a nice hotel, and it was (5) ______ a short walk to the beach! We went there every day. And in the winter, everything is (6) ______ cheap! We had (7) ______ a great time and we want to go again.

3 **Underline the best way to complete the sentences.**

a The beach was very crowded, but we **couldn't find a place to sit / had a great afternoon.**
b The architecture is too modern and I really **don't like it / like it.**
c The stores were very expensive, but we **bought a lot of things / bought nothing.**
d Our hotel room was too small, so **it wasn't a problem / we asked for another one.**
e They arrived at the airport very late, but they **caught their plane / didn't catch their plane.**
f You're driving too fast and **I'm enjoying it / you're breaking the law.**
g I know our town is very dull, but we're **happy there / not happy there.**
h The ocean was too cold, so we **didn't go swimming / went swimming.**

4 **Complete the sentences with *much* or *many*.**

a I don't have __much__ work to do today.
b I don't have ______ friends, unfortunately.
c I get too ______ emails every day.
d I ate too ______ chocolate yesterday.
e I don't know how ______ people live in my town.
f I often wear way too ______ perfume.
g I haven't seen ______ American movies.
h I don't drink ______ coffee.

5 **Rewrite the sentences so that they are true for you.**

a I have a lot of work to do today.
b ______
c ______
d ______
e ______
f ______
g ______
h ______

6 <u>Underline</u> the correct alternative.

a How <u>much</u> / **many** do you know about Los Angeles?
b In two days, you do not have **enough** / **little** time to see everything.
c There are **a little** / **a lot of** big houses in Hollywood.
d There are **much** / **not enough** parks in the city.
e There is way **a lot of** / **too much** traffic in the city.
f **Much** / **Not many** people in Los Angeles speak languages other than English.
g Los Angeles only gets **a little** / **not enough** rain in the summer.
h **A few** / **Many** police officers have guns.

Now decide if sentences (b–h) are true (T) or false (F).

7 **Match the sentences (a–g) with their responses (1–7).**

a Would you like some sugar in that coffee?
b Do we have a lot of time?
c I'm sorry, but I don't have enough money.
d She's got a lot of friends.
e The metro system is really up-to-date.
f We don't get enough homework.
g Are there any good restaurants in your town?

1 But there aren't enough trains.
2 Here, take a little from my wallet.
3 No, not much.
4 Not enough? Way too much!
5 Yes, a few. But they're expensive.
6 Yes, but not many good ones.
7 Yes, please. Just a little.

a	b	c	d	e	f	g
7						

Vocabulary

1 **Complete the sentences with the words in the box.**

beach	canal	fountain
high-rise	hill	library
square	~~statue~~	

a Have you seen the __statue__ of Shakespeare outside the theater?
b Let's go swimming at the __________.
c On Saturdays, there is a market in the large __________ downtown.
d The park is on a __________ and has good views of the city.
e I like sitting near the bridge over the __________ and watching all the boats.
f They have an office in one of the __________ buildings not far from the station.
g Children enjoy playing in the water of the __________.
h Many people go to the __________ not for the books, but to use the computers.

2 <u>Underline</u> the correct adjective.

Bangkok is one of the most (1) <u>exciting</u> / **quiet** cities in the world. It's (2) **big** / **great**, with a population of over ten million. A (3) **big** / **great** way to see the city is to take a boat along the Chao Phraya River. From there, you have (4) **fantastic** / **friendly** views of the old city with the (5) **cheap** / **spectacular** royal palace and many (6) **beautiful** / **dull** temples. The people are very (7) **expensive** / **friendly** and (8) **polluted** / **welcoming.**

The center of the city is (9) **beautiful** / **modern** with hundreds of high-rise buildings and shopping malls. The streets are (10) **crowded** / **romantic** and with so many cars, it's (11) **fabulous** / **noisy** and (12) **polluted** / **spectacular**. In some months, it is also very hot and (13) **humid** / **up-to-date.** But one thing you can say about Bangkok is that it's never (14) **dull** / **hot**! If you love shopping, it's a (15) **fabulous** / **humid** place to be and it's not (16) **expensive** / **lovely.** The markets in China Town are very (17) **cheap** / **freezing**, and don't leave without a visit to the (18) **boring** / **romantic** night market.

3 **Complete the sentences with a country adjective.**

a A sombrero is a M__exican__ hat.
b Fuji is a J__________ mountain.
c Spaghetti is an I__________ dish.
d Valparaíso is a C__________ city.
e Lisbon is the P__________ capital.
f The Great Pyramid is an E__________ monument.
g Samba and Bossa Nova are kinds of B__________ music.
h Juan Péron was an A__________ president.
i The C__________ flag is red and white with a red leaf.

4 **Label the rooms with the words in the boxes.**

bathroom	bedroom	dining room
kitchen	~~living room~~	

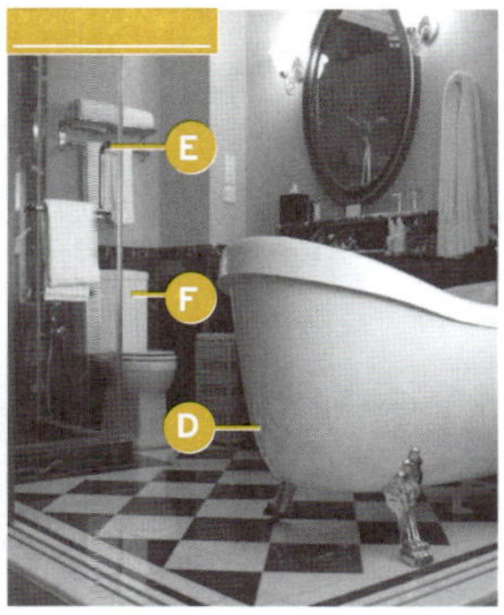

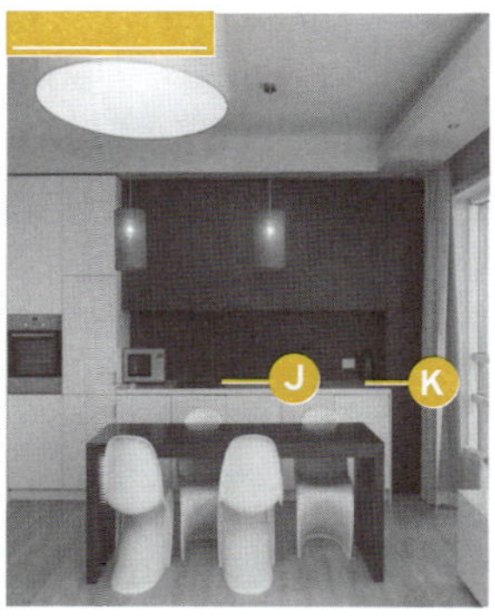

rug	bathtub	bed
chair	couch	lamp
shower	sink	stove
table	toilet	desk
~~TV~~		

A TV
B ______
C ______
D ______
E ______
F ______
G ______
H ______
I ______
J ______
K ______
L ______
M ______

5 **Read the description of Sicily and complete the labels (a–h).**

Most of the cities and large towns of Sicily are on the coast. The biggest city, Palermo, is on the north coast in the west of the island. The second-biggest city, Catania, is in the middle of the east coast, and the third, Messina, where most travelers arrive from Italy, is in the north-east corner. Siracusa, with its beautiful palaces, is also on the east coast, but further south than Catania. Agrigento, with its famous Greek monuments, is in the middle of the south-west coast. Ragusa, the biggest town that is not on the coast, is in the south-east corner of the island. In the mountains in the center of Sicily is the beautiful town of Enna. The famous volcano, Mount Etna, is in the north-east, between Messina and Catania.

a Palermo
b ______
c ______
d ______
e ______
f ______
g ______
h ______

Pronunciation

1 **Circle the word in each group that has a different vowel sound from the others.**

a (come) most only smoke
b crowded flower fountain neighbor
c choice money noisy royal
d home hotel honey road

05 **Listen and check.**

2 **Look at the words in the box. Is the underlined sound /oʊ/, /aʊ/, or /ɔɪ/? Put the words in the correct column.**

~~boy~~	~~coast~~	coin	don't
enjoy	hotel	~~how~~	most
noise	noun	outside	phone
south	town	voice	

/oʊ/	/aʊ/	/ɔɪ/
coast	how	boy

06 **Listen and check. Repeat the words.**

Listening

1 07 Cover the listening script. Listen to the recording. Which place is the speaker describing?

a

b

c

I guess the best place I've ever been is Marrakech. It's such an interesting and exciting city. I first went there many years ago, maybe ten, twelve years, I can't remember exactly. I was living and working in Casablanca, which is, oh, I don't know, about four or five hours from Marrakech. We had a long weekend, and Dave and I – he was my best friend at the time – were looking for something to do. There was a guy we worked with, Malik, and he invited us to come and stay with his family.

So we all left Casablanca on a Thursday evening after work, and we got to Marrakech that night. Malik's family lives in a fantastic house very close to the main square with the market, Djemaa el Fna. His mother cooked us dinner and then we all went to the square. We sat on the roof of a café, drinking mint tea, and watching the people in the square below us. It really is such an incredible place! There are people buying and selling absolutely everything. There are lots of little kitchens, serving soup and kebabs, and other things to eat. You can listen to storytellers (if you speak Arabic, that is), watch snake charmers, acrobats, and so on.

There's so much to see and do. The Koutoubia Mosque is spectacular and all the tourists go there. The views are fabulous, with the Atlas Mountains in the distance, and there are some beautiful parks, like the garden that belonged to Yves St. Laurent.

But it's the square, the Djemaa el Fna, and the shopping streets around it, that make Marrakech really special. Every time I go back to Marrakech, and I've probably been there ten or twelve times, I go straight to the square and sit at my favorite café. If I ever have the money, I'd love to buy a house there. But right now, I don't even have a job, and the last time I went there was three years ago.

2 Listen again. Are the statements true (T) or false (F)?

a He first went to Marrakech five years ago. F
b He went there for his summer vacation. _____
c He traveled with his girlfriend. _____
d He stayed with the family of a friend. _____
e After dinner, he visited a mosque. _____
f Djemaa el Fna is the name of a good café. _____
g There is a lot to see in the main square. _____
h You can see the mountains from the city. _____
i He has been there six times. _____
j His last visit was three months ago. _____

Correct the statements that are false.

a ____________________
b ____________________
c ____________________
d ____________________
e ____________________
f ____________________
g ____________________
h ____________________
i ____________________
j ____________________

3 Love

Grammar

1 **Find 14 irregular simple past words in the wordsquare. Look → and ↓.**

G	L	E	C	M	N	R	C	M	X	Z	E	P	I	U	B	H	P	H	E	N	Y	S	M	V
Y	E	D	U	U	K	H	U	B	Q	Q	S	B	E	G	A	N	I	S	K	I	B	X	E	R
Q	G	R	T	K	I	M	U	I	R	H	E	A	W	M	Q	V	E	I	W	A	L	X	T	R
U	Q	M	M	N	D	X	X	C	I	L	U	H	C	Z	Z	N	R	H	O	P	U	T	W	S
S	B	K	E	A	R	F	H	J	J	G	G	O	P	Y	A	I	U	E	J	S	V	U	B	M
L	V	S	Z	P	A	C	P	N	T	X	U	A	I	P	G	T	S	W	A	M	I	S	R	B
E	E	N	N	D	N	Y	H	L	H	U	T	O	A	N	H	A	U	V	E	G	M	H	O	G
P	L	I	Z	A	K	B	U	I	O	S	R	J	K	F	G	L	H	K	D	A	Q	R	U	Y
T	O	O	K	W	M	C	S	T	U	A	O	C	A	U	G	H	T	X	Z	M	I	P	G	G
G	Q	Y	R	N	I	R	N	F	G	A	P	G	M	K	V	A	F	V	S	B	M	A	H	R
O	C	S	V	Y	W	X	E	H	H	C	M	D	V	C	A	N	U	D	R	Z	T	L	T	R
A	C	A	M	E	Y	G	F	G	T	E	R	Z	F	C	T	A	U	G	H	T	N	N	U	K

2 **Match the simple past verbs in the wordsquare in Exercise 1 with the infinitives.**

a begin *began*
b bring ______
c catch ______
d come ______
e cut ______
f drink ______
g put ______
h light ______
i meet ______
j sleep ______
k swim ______
l take ______
m teach ______
n think ______

3 **Write the words in the correct order to make questions.**

a Did go shopping yesterday you ?
Did you go shopping yesterday?

b cold it Was yesterday ?
______

c Did enjoy vacation last you your ?
______

d English last class was When your ?
______

e did go vacation last on Where year you ?
______

f did dinner for have last night What you ?
______

g in best friends elementary school were Who your ?
______

Write true answers to the questions.

4 Write the sentences in the negative.

a Juliet was a happy girl.
Juliet wasn't a happy girl.

b Juliet's family and Romeo's family were friends.
______

c They wanted her to marry him.
______

d Juliet was in love with Paris, a friend of her family.
______

e She liked him.
______

f Juliet knew what to do.
______

g She told her parents about her true feelings.
______

5 **Look at the picture of a modern Romeo and Juliet. Complete the sentences with verbs from the box in the past progressive.**

feel	get	hold
plan	sit	speak
~~wear~~		

a Juliet *was wearing* an old T-shirt.
b She ______ a cup of coffee.
c It was late and she ______ tired.
d Romeo ______ on his motorcycle.
e They ______ on their cell phones.
f Romeo ______ wet.
g They ______ to get married.

6 **Put the verbs in parentheses into the correct form. Use the simple past or the past progressive.**

Juliet (1) __was going__ (go) out with a man named Paris, but she didn't love him. One evening, she (2) ______________ (watch) TV when her cell phone rang. It was Romeo and he (3) ______________ (say) that he was in her street. She (4) ______________ (open) the door of the balcony and saw him. He (5) ______________ (sit) on a motorcycle. When he saw her, he (6) ______________ (begin) to sing. It was a beautiful song and Juliet (7) ______________ (want) it to last forever. But it (8) ______________ (rain) and she was cold. She (9) ______________ (decide) to ask Romeo inside. Then, another motorcycle (10) ______________ (arrive). It was Paris ...

7 **Make adverbs from the adjectives.**

a regular __regularly__
b attractive __________
c beautiful __________
d early __________
e fast __________
f happy __________
g loud __________

8 **Underline the correct alternative.**

a Be careful / **carefully** if you swim in the ocean!
b I play soccer very **bad** / **badly**, but I enjoy it.
c Could you speak more **quiet** / **quietly** please?
d She wrote the note very **quick** / **quickly**.
e Their house is always very **neat** / **neatly**.
f He was **angry** / **angrily** and wanted revenge.
g She knows me very **good** / **well**.
h We're sisters but we look very **different** / **differently**.

Vocabulary

1 **Complete the story with the words in the box.**

called	date	flirt
have	kissed	~~liked~~
meet	was	

I saw a boy at a party that I (1) __liked__ and I decided to (2) __________ with him. I (3) __________ him the next day and we began to (4) __________ each other. After three weeks, he finally (5) __________ me. He said that he (6) __________ in love with me. He wanted to (7) __________ lots of children and he wanted me to (8) __________ his parents.

2 **Continue the story in Exercise 1 with the words in the box.**

get	had	~~live~~
lost	move	split

I said, "Maybe it's a good idea to (1) __live__ together first, before starting a family."
"I don't want to (2) __________ in together before we (3) __________ married," he replied. That was when we (4) __________ our first and last fight. Two days later, we (5) __________ up and I completely (6) __________ touch with him.

3 **Cross out the response that is *not* possible.**

a **A:** I think Johnny Depp's so good-looking.
B: ~~Oh, I do.~~ / Oh, I don't. / So do I.

b **A:** I got really bored.
B: Neither did I. / Oh, I didn't. / So did I.

c **A:** I didn't understand the book.
B: Me, neither / Neither did I. / Oh, I didn't.

d **A:** I'm not married.
B: Me, neither. / Me, too. / Neither am I.

4 **Underline the best alternative from the options below to complete the text.**

1 At first / One day / That day
2 At first / Next / The next morning
3 Finally / Last week / Then
4 A week later / Next / That evening
5 At the end of the month / Finally / One day
6 Last night / Last year / That night
7 A week later / The next morning / That night

(1) __One day__ a man was talking to his wife when she stopped him and said, "Do you know tomorrow is our wedding anniversary? We got married twenty years ago." (2) __________, he didn't believe her. "No," he replied, "it's next month, isn't it?" "No, tomorrow," she said. (3) __________ she continued, "You forgot, and now I want a really special gift."

(4) __________, the man thought for a long time about a gift for his wife. He had lots of ideas, but he could not decide. (5) __________, he decided to ask his wife. "Would you like to go shopping in New York?" he said. "No, not that. Something special," she said. "How about a new car?" he suggested.
"No. I want something really special," she replied.
(6) __________ he went to bed and he still had no idea what to give his wife.

(7) __________, he got up and wrote a check to his wife for $100,000. "Happy Anniversary," he said and gave her the check. "I don't want money," she said. "I want something really, really special. I want a divorce!"

"Sorry, too expensive," he replied

08 **Listen and check.**

5 **Label the pictures with the adjectives in the box.**

annoyed	bored	confused
embarrassed	~~relaxed~~	scared
surprised	tired	

a

relaxed

e

____

b

____

f

____

c

____

g

____

d

____

h

____

6 **Check (✓) the best way to continue the sentences.**

a Why are you so bored? ...
- [ ] Do something original!
- [x] Don't you like the movie?

b My mother was so embarrassing! ...
- [ ] She talked about me when I was a child.
- [ ] Her face went really red.

c He looked really scary. ...
- [ ] He was wearing a Dracula costume.
- [ ] I said I had a snake in my bag.

d The children were very tired. ...
- [ ] They wanted to play all the time.
- [ ] They had a late night last night.

e The teacher was a little confusing. ...
- [ ] He couldn't remember anybody's name.
- [ ] He was very hard to understand.

f I thought she was very interested. ...
- [ ] She told some very good stories.
- [ ] She wanted a lot more information.

7 **Complete the sentences with the words in the box.**

along	tickets	better
changed	dark	divorced
together	~~to work~~	

a There was a lot of traffic, so we got to work very late.

b In the summer it gets __________ much later.

c I thought the movie got __________ near the end.

d Many unhappy couples don't get __________ because of the children.

e My old college friends and I get __________ every year.

f We got __________ to the Taylor Swift concert.

g I hope you're going to get __________ before we go out this evening.

h She doesn't get __________ very well with her parents.

Pronunciation

1 09 **Listen and notice the different pronunciations of *was* and *were*.**

	was	*were*
Usual pronunciation	Short /wəz/	Short /wər/
Pronunciation in short answers	Long /wɑz/	Long /wɜr/

A: What were you doing at eight o'clock?

B: I was having breakfast.

A: And your wife? Was she having breakfast, too?

B: Yes, she was. We both were.

2 **Look at *was* and *were* in the conversation and write the correct phonetic symbols (/wəz/ or /wɑz/, /wər/ or /wɜr/) in the boxes.**

A: What were you doing when you met?

a [ ]

B: I was working as a nurse.

b [ ]

A: Where did you meet? Was it at the hospital?

c [ ]

B: Yes, it was.

d [ ]

A: Were you both single at the time?

e [ ]

B: Yes, we were.

f [ ]

10 **Listen and check. Then practice saying the phrases.**

Writing

Linking sentences with *after/before* + *ing*
Writing a story

1 **Read the beginning of the story of Bonnie and Clyde and number the pictures in the correct order (1–3).**

Before becoming a famous bank robber, Bonnie Parker worked in a café. One day, a good-looking young man, Clyde Barrow, walked into the café. It was love at first sight. They talked and, after finishing the meal, the two left the café together.

The next day, they were walking along the street together when they saw a car that Bonnie liked. "Let's take it," she said. Clyde agreed. He fixed the motor and the couple drove out of town.

They drove for a few miles and then realized that they needed gas. They stopped at a garage and asked the attendant to fill the car.

A

☐

B

☐

C

☐

2 **Look at the examples. Then link the pairs of sentences (a–e).**

Bonnie Parker worked in a café. Later she became a famous bank robber.

Before becom*ing* a famous bank robber, Bonnie Parker worked in a café.

He finished the meal. Then they left the café together.
After finish*ing* the meal, they left the café.

a They stole a car. Then they drove out of town.
After stealing a car, they drove out of town.

b They drove for a few miles. Then they realized they needed gas.
After ______________________

c They filled the car with gas. Then they killed the garage attendant.
Before ______________________

d They stole money from the garage. They drove away.
Before ______________________

3 **Look at the pictures and answer the questions to complete the story.**

Where did Bonnie and Clyde go one week later?
What did they do there?

What did they do before leaving the bank?

What were Bonnie and Clyde doing six months later?
Where were the police officers?
Who were they waiting for?
What happened next? (Use your imagination!)

4 Shopping

Grammar

1 **Write the adverbs in the correct part of the table.**

~~always~~	hardly ever	never
normally	occasionally	often
rarely	sometimes	usually

100% always
______
______ ______
______ ______
______ ______
0% ______

2 **Write the words in the correct order.**

a a always am diet I on
I am always on a diet.

b ever hardly I perfume wear
______

c buy clothes I often second-hand
______

d don't gold I jewelry like usually
______

e a is pleasure rarely Shopping
______

f after always changed I get work
______

g are dirty My shoes sometimes
______

h am at choosing good I normally gifts
______

Change the sentences so they are true for you.

a *I am rarely on a diet.*
b ______
c ______
d ______
e ______
f ______
g ______
h ______

3 **Complete the sentences with *for* or *to*.**

a I think I'll buy some perfume *for* *my grandmother.*
b I told a story ______ *the children.*
c I lent my car ______ *my sister.*
d He made a delicious meal ______ *his girlfriend.*
e Why don't you get some chocolate ______ *your mother?*
f He showed his wedding album ______ *his boss.*
g Give the ticket ______ *your neighbor.*
h I sent an email ______ *the bank manager* last week.

4 **Rewrite the sentences in Exercise 3. Replace the words in italics with a pronoun (*him*, *her*, *it*, *them*), and do not use *for* or *to*.**

a *I think I'll buy her some perfume.*
b ______
c ______
d ______
e ______
f ______
g ______
h ______

5 **Underline the correct verb form.**

a I can't stand <u>cooking</u> / to cook.
b I didn't choose **studying / to study** English.
c I didn't manage **finishing / to finish** my homework last night.
d I enjoy **spending / to spend** time with my parents.
e I never refuse **lending / to lend** money to my friends.
f I often forget **taking off / to take off** my earrings when I go to bed.
g I usually avoid **going / to go** to the store on Saturdays.
h I would like **having / to have** six children.

Check (✓) the sentences that are true for you.

6 **Complete the conversation with the correct form of the verbs in the box. Use the *-ing* form or the *to*-infinitive.**

be	choose	eat	get	go
spend	talk	~~try~~	watch	

A: I want (1) __to try__ these on. Do you mind (2)________ my bag for a few minutes?

B: OK, but please don't spend all afternoon (3)________ a dress. I love (4) ________ time with you, honey, but we agreed (5) ________ to only two or three stores.

A: I know, but I want (6) ________ something really nice.

B: But I like everything you buy, and we need (7) ________ careful with money.

A: Oh, I hate (8) ________ about money. If we can afford (9) ________ at expensive restaurants, we can afford one little dress!

11 **Listen and check.**

7 **Complete the questions with the simple present or present progressive form of the verbs in parentheses.**

a __Do you come__ (you come) from a large family?

b ______________ (you listen) to the radio right now?

c ______________ (most of your friends work) in an office?

d ______________ (it rain) a lot in your town in winter?

e ______________ (the students in your class study) for examinations?

f ______________ (you read) a newspaper every day?

g ______________ (your father) speak English?

h ______________ (it get) dark right now?

Write true answers to the questions.

Vocabulary

1 **Match the words on the left with those on the right.**

a	a can of	gum
b	a bunch of	cake
c	a box of	grapes
d	a pair of	matches
e	a pack of	mayonnaise
f	a piece of	perfume
g	a bottle of	paint
h	a jar of	scissors

2 **Label the designs below. The first and last letters have been done for you.**

a patterned

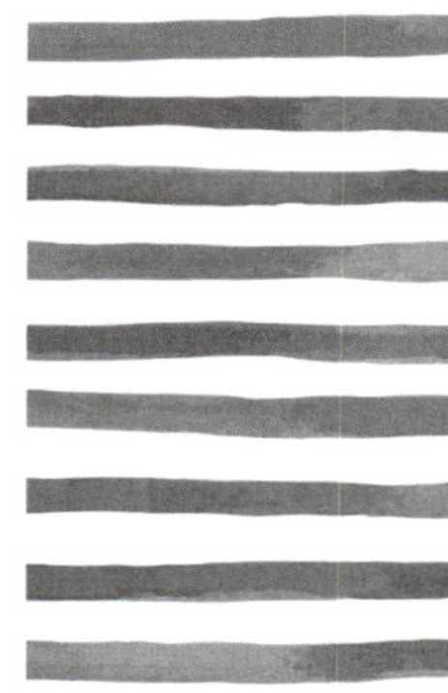

d s_ _ _ _ _ _d

b f_ _ _ _ _l

e c_ _ _ _ _ _d

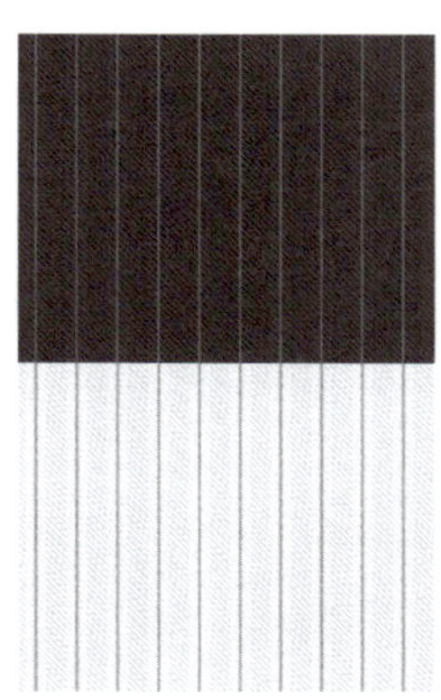

c p_ _ _ _ _ _ _ _ _d

f p_ _ _n

3 Match the questions (a–h) with their answers (1–8).

a Can I help you?
b What are you looking for?
c What colors do you have?
d How would you like to pay?
e What size is he?
f What do you think? Do you like it?
g Can I exchange it?
h How much is it?

1 By credit card, if that's OK.
2 I'm looking for something for my girlfriend, actually.
3 Large, or maybe extra large.
4 No, I'm just looking, thank you.
5 It's 49.99.
6 We only have it in purple, I'm afraid.
7 Yes, it's great. I'll take it.
8 Yes, of course. Make sure you keep the receipt.

a	b	c	d	e	f	g	h
4							

4 Match the words in the box with the pictures below.

dress	gloves	hat
~~jacket~~	pajamas	pantyhose
coat	scarf	shirt
shoes	skirt	suit
tie		

a ______ jacket ______

c ______ ______ ______

b ______

d ______ ______ ______

e ______ ______ ______

Pronunciation

1 Look at the words in the box. Is the underlined sound /eɪ/or/aɪ/? Put the words in the correct column.

~~always~~	brain	~~decide~~
exchange	great	mind
pay	plain	right
same	striped	style
surprise	try	

/eɪ/	/aɪ/
always	decide

12 Listen and check. Repeat the words.

2 Look at the ad. Underline the words that contain the /eɪ/ sound. Circle the words that contain the /aɪ/ sound.

13 Listen and check.

Listening

1 14 **Cover the listening script and listen to a news report about the movie premiere of *Spider-Man: Homecoming*.**

What are the speakers talking about?

a Critical opinions of the movie
b The plot (story) of the movie
c The stars of the movie and their clothes

Michael: Millions of fans around the world are waiting for the new *Spider-Man* movie, but here in Los Angeles, we are very lucky. Today is the world premiere of *Spider-Man: Homecoming*. The movie cost a hundred and seventy-five million dollars to make, and the stars will be visiting different cities around the world for the premieres. Next week they will be in London, but for tonight they are here in LA. We sent Claire Chadwick to Hollywood to find out what's happening. Claire, can you hear me?

Claire: Yes, Michael. I'm standing here in Hollywood, outside the TCL Chinese Theater, and thousands of people are waiting to see the stars of the new *Spider-Man* movie. Many of them are wearing *Spider-Man* clothes and people are very, very excited.

You can hear the cheers and the shouting, and the first stars are beginning to arrive. Someone is getting out of the car just in front of me. It's – who is it? I think it's – no it's Karen Gillan, the Scottish actress. She's walking on the red carpet now and she's wearing a beautiful blue velvet dress.

Over there I can see Jason Derulo and that's Isabel Moner. And now it's Zendaya, one of the main stars of the movie. She's getting out of her car now. Who's she with? Ah ... it's her mom! And now she's going over to the fans, and she's signing autographs. She's wearing a beautiful pink dress – she looks absolutely fantastic.

Oh, and now I can see Tom Holland. He's standing next to another group of fans. He's wearing a stylish black suit, white shirt, and tie. He looks like a businessman. And the screams are getting louder. Michael, I think it's time to go back to you in the studio.

2 **Listen again and check (✓) the correct answer.**

1 How much did *Spider-Man: Homecoming* cost to make?
a $150 million
b $175 million
c $200 million

2 Where was the world premiere of *Spider-Man: Homecoming*?
a London
b New York
c Los Angeles

3 Who was the first star to arrive?
a Karen Gillan
b Zendaya
c Isabel Monder

4 Who was Zendaya with?
a her boyfriend
b her mom
c Tom Holland

5 What was Zendaya wearing?
a a blue velvet dress
b a *Spider-Man* costume
c a pink dress

6 What was Tom Holland wearing?
a a red suit
b a black suit
c a *Spider-Man* costume

5 In shape

Grammar

1 **Complete the table.**

Adjective	Comparative	Superlative
good	better	best
near	______	______
wet	______	______
easy	______	______
far	______	______
dangerous	______	______

2 **Complete the sentences.**

a Skiing is more dangerous than basketball.
Basketball isn't as dangerous as skiing.

b Tennis is more interesting than judo.
Judo isn't ______.

c Men aren't as good as women at ball games.
Women are ______.

d Running is better for you than swimming.
Swimming is not ______.

e The rules of volleyball are not as easy to understand as the rules of basketball.
The rules of basketball are ______.

f Watching a sport is more exciting than playing it.
Playing a sport is not ______.

g Being in shape is not as important for older people as it is for younger people.
Being in shape is ______.

Do you agree with the statements above? Change them, if necessary, so that they are true for you.

3 **Complete the sentences with the superlative form of the adjectives in the box.**

big	crowded	expensive
fast	~~heavy~~	hot
noisy	wet	

a The heaviest animal is the blue whale, which weighs about twenty-six tons.

b ______ island in the world is Greenland (2 million km²).

c ______ country in the world is Monaco, with more than 16,000 people per square kilometer.

d With 12 meters of rain every year, Kauai Island in Hawaii is ______ place in the world.

e ______ planet is Venus, with a temperature of about 460°C.

f Oslo, where most things cost more than Paris or London, is ______ city in Europe.

g Howler monkeys are ______ animals in the world: you can hear their cries from five kilometers away.

h After doing 50 meters in under 21 seconds, César Cielo became ______ swimmer in the world.

4 **Insert the missing words in the text below. Use the words in the box.**

as	as	as
more	~~most~~	than
than	the	the

The ^most dangerous age for a man's health is from 50 to 60. Exercise is very important, but not important as a healthy diet. A bad diet is biggest reason for health problems. Vegetables are better fast food, for example. People with most stressful jobs have a shorter life people who have no stress. They should try to relax. They should exercise than once a week. A hard, sweaty sport is not good for your health regular, easy exercise.

15 **Listen and check.**

5 **Write the words in the correct order to complete the questions.**

a given has coffee up
Do you know anyone who has given up coffee?

b clothes hang up your
Do you always __________ in the evening?

c deal problems with
Do you always __________ immediately?

d words up look
How often do you __________ in the dictionary?

e a care of baby taken
Have you ever __________?

f a filled form in
When was the last time that you __________?

g away love letters old throw
Do you ever __________?

h an excuse make up
Do you ever __________ when you're late?

i get along people the with
How do you __________ in your class?

Write true answers to the questions.

6 **Rewrite the sentences by replacing the words in italics with the pronoun in parentheses.**

a Don't forget to turn off *the light*. (it)
Don't forget to turn it off.

b I take after *my father*. (him)
____

c My grandparents brought up *my sister*. (her)
____

d He decided to give up *swimming*. (it)
____

e Please put away *your books*. (them)
____

f The children cleared up *the mess*. (it)
____

g We had to call off *the party*. (it)
____

Vocabulary

1 **Match the questions (a–h) with the answers (1–8).**

a How far is the closest bus stop from your school?
b How fast can you run 100 meters?
c How long does it take you to get dressed in the morning?
d How many people are there in your family?
e How much homework do you have today?
f How often do you go swimming?
g How old is your car?
h How well can you speak Chinese?

1 About ten minutes.
2 About two hundred meters.
3 Four, but with me, it's five.
4 I'm not sure. Fifteen seconds, maybe.
5 I've had it for three years.
6 Not a lot. Two or three exercises.
7 Not as well as my mother.
8 Never. I can't stand it.

a	b	c	d	e	f	g	h
2							

Write true answers to the questions.

2 **Complete the questions with an adjective or an adverb.**

a How fast can you learn to speak a foreign language?
b How __________ can you play golf?
c How __________ do you go on vacation?
d How __________ does it cost?
e How __________ does it take you to get to school?
f How __________ is it to the station?
g How __________ is your brother?
h How __________ people are there in your classroom?

3 **Underline the correct way of saying the numbers.**

a 500 five hundred / five hundreds
b 0.5 nil point five / point five
c ¾ three quarter / three quarters
d 1.75 one point seven five / one point seventy five
e 7,184 seven thousand, one hundred and eighty-four / seventy-one hundred, eight four
f 3–0 three–nil / three–oh
g 1½ one and half / one and a half

4 **Cross out the word that is *not* possible.**

a He decided to give up **coffee** / ~~**his neighbors**~~ / **sugar**.

b Where can I hang up my **coat** / **clothes** / **shoes**?

c He put on a **car** / **suit** / **tie** to go to work.

d She got home and turned on a **novel** / **the computer** / **the TV**.

e She took off her **hat** / **keys** / **shoes** when she entered the house.

f I never throw away **old newspapers** / **plastic bags** / **the office**.

5 **Complete the definitions with the phrasal verbs in the box.**

bring up	clear up	deal with
fill in	get along with	look up
~~run after~~	take after	

a If you *run after* someone or something, you follow it very quickly.

b When you _____ something _____, you make it neat by organizing things.

c If you _____ a problem, you do something to find a solution.

d When you _____ a form, you write information in the empty spaces.

e If you _____ someone, you look like someone in your family (mother, father, or grandparents).

f If you _____ someone, you have a good relationship with them.

g When you _____ a child, you take care of them until they are an adult.

h If you _____ something _____, you try to find information about it in a book.

6 **Put the words in the box into the correct group.**

court	field	goggles
~~golf~~	golfer	helmet
net	runner	skier
skiing	soccer	swimming pool

a Sports:

golf _____ _____

b People:

_____ _____ _____

c Places:

_____ _____ _____

d Equipment:

_____ _____ _____

7 **What could you say in these situations? Choose an expression from the box.**

Be careful!	Be patient.	Come back!
~~Don't be mean!~~	Don't worry.	Try again.

a You show your new dress to a friend. Your friend laughs and says that you look like a waitress.
You say: *Don't be mean!*

b A friend tells you that they have an important exam next week. They say that it is very difficult.
You say: _____

c You are in a subway station and a train arrives. Your friend goes to get on the train, but you suddenly realize that you have left your bag at the ticket office.
You say: _____

d You are with a friend and waiting for another friend to arrive. Your friend is getting angry because the other one is ten minutes late.
You say: _____

e You are with a friend. Your friend calls a restaurant to reserve a table, but the line is busy.
You say: _____

f You are in a car with your friend who is driving. Your friend is driving a little fast.
You say: _____

8 **Complete the text with *does*, *goes*, or *plays*.**

Tyler is very serious about sports. In the morning, he usually (1) *goes* cycling, but he sometimes (2) _____ swimming at the pool. At work, he (3) _____ exercises during his coffee breaks and he occasionally (4) _____ golf in his office! At lunchtime, he (5) _____ tennis or squash. Then, in the evenings, he (6) _____ judo for an hour or two at the gym. On the weekend, he also (7) _____ as many sports as possible. He (8) _____ baseball on Saturdays and soccer on Sundays. For vacations, he (9) _____ skiing in the winter and windsurfing in the summer.

▶ 16 **Listen and check.**

Writing

Organizing a text
Linking sentences with *although*
Describing a sports event

1 Look at the plan and put the paragraphs (A, B, C) in the correct order.

1 name, title, place of the event
Paragraph _____

2 description of the event
Paragraph _____

3 feelings, comments, final thoughts
Paragraph _____

A I arrived early because I didn't want to miss anything. Although my seat was far back, I still had a great view. Caroline Wozniacki won the first match. It was really exciting, although Wozniacki was much stronger than her opponent. Then Venus was up against Timea Bacsinszky. Although Williams won the first set, she lost the next two and Bacsinszky won the match. Later, I watched Novak Djokovic play against Albert Ramos Viñolas. I wanted Ramos Viñolas to win because he's Spanish, like me. But unfortunately, he also lost his match.

B This was my first visit to Roland Garros. Although I was glad that I saw some of my favorite players, it was a shame that they lost their matches. I would love to go again ... hopefully to see them win!

C The French Open tennis championships take place in May and June every year at the Roland Garros stadium in Paris. This year, a friend gave me a ticket for the eighth day of the competition. When I discovered that I was going to watch Venus Williams, I was thrilled. She's my hero!

2 Match the sentence beginnings (a–g) with their endings (1–7).

a Although I was pleased to see my favorite players, 5
b Although I love tennis,
c Although Venus won the first set,
d Although Bacsinszky won this match,
e Many people prefer watching the men's matches,
f Some tickets are very cheap,
g The tournament's official name is Roland Garros,

1 although it is often called The French Open.
2 although the women's matches are often more exciting.
3 although the most expensive cost more than 200 euros.
4 she lost the match.
5 it was a shame that they lost their matches.
6 she lost in the semifinals.
7 this was my first visit to a major championship.

3 Link the sentences with *although*.

a We arrived early. There was a very long line.
Although we arrived early, there was a very long line.

b The tickets were very expensive. We didn't have a very good view.
____

c The match was very exciting. It was very long.
____

d Nothing much happened in the first half. The second half was fantastic.
____

e Chivas won the game. They were not the better team.
____

f I enjoyed the game. My friends thought it was boring.
____

4 Write a description of a sports event that you have attended. Use the paragraph plan in Exercise 1.

Pronunciation

1 The words in each group have the same vowel sound. Insert the missing letters. Choose from the letters in the boxes.

-ir-	-or-	-ur-

f i r s t	w i n d s ______ f
t h ______ d	w ______ k
t ______ n	w ______ st

-or-	-our-

c ______ s e	s p ______ t
c ______ t	m ______ e
s c ______ e	f ______

▶ 17 **Listen and repeat the words.**

2 Look at the words in the box. Is the underlined sound /ɜr/ or /ɔr/? Put the words in the correct column.

~~board~~	~~earn~~	form
morning	person	serve
story	thirst	

/ɜr/	/ɔr/
earn	*board*
______	______
______	______
______	______

▶ 18 **Listen and check. Repeat the words.**

6 Job

Grammar

1 **Match each group of sentences (1–2) with a job in the box.**

an au pair	a DJ
a model	a flight attendant

1 She has to wear a uniform at work.
She can travel to different countries for free.
She doesn't have to have a college education.
She can't sit down much in her job.
She is ________________.

2 She doesn't have to pay for somewhere to live.
She can wear her own clothes.
She has to like young children.
She can't invite her friends to dinner.
She is ________________.

2 **Change the eight sentences in Exercise 1 to questions.**

a *Does she have to wear a uniform at work?*
b ________________
c ________________
d ________________
e ________________
f ________________
g ________________
h ________________

3 **Think of a woman you know. Answer the questions in Exercise 2.**

a *Yes, she does. / No, she doesn't.*
b ________________
c ________________
d ________________
e ________________
f ________________
g ________________
h ________________

4 **Complete the sentences with the present perfect form of the verbs in parentheses.**

a How many different jobs *has she had* (she had)?
b She ____________ (have) lots of different jobs in her life.
c ____________ (you ever work) in a factory?
d No, I ____________ (never be) in a bakery.
e What's the worst meal you ____________ (ever eat)?
f I ____________ (like) most of my jobs and I like this one, too.
g Yes, I ____________ (always want) to be a ballet dancer.

5 **Write questions for the answers below.**

a *Have you ever been on TV?*
No, I've never been on TV.
b ________________
No, I've never worked as an au pair.
c ________________
No, my parents have never forgotten my birthday.
d ________________
No, my teacher has never made a joke in class.
e ________________
No, I've never seen a ballet.
f ________________
No, I've never voted in a political election.
g ________________
No, I've never ridden a motorcycle.

Write true answers to the questions above.

6 Put the verbs in parentheses in the correct form. Use the simple past or the present perfect.

I (1) __have had__ (have) lots of horrible jobs in my life, but the worst job I (2) ___________ (ever have) was selling hot dogs.

I (3) ___________ (start) the job at the beginning of last summer because I (4) ___________ (need) some money to buy a car. It was the biggest mistake I (5) ___________ (ever make) in my life. I (6) ___________ (not like) the smell of the hot dogs and, on the first day, I (7) ___________ (feel) sick. The weather (8) ___________ (be) really bad and I only (9) ___________ (sell) two or three. At the end of the day, the boss (10) __________ (say) to me, "You (11) ___________ (no sell) enough!"

The next morning, I (12) ___________ (decide) to stay in bed.

19 **Listen and check.**

7 **Underline the correct time expression.**

a I learned to drive **ever** / **in my life** / **when I was eighteen**.
b I haven't been to the movies **a few weeks ago** / **last week** / **this week**.
c I bought a beautiful dress **in my life** / **over the years** / **yesterday**.
d I didn't go to the beach at all **last summer** / **over the years** / **recently**.
e I've been to a few good restaurants **last Friday** / **recently** / **years ago**.
f I've spent way too much money **last night** / **today** / **yesterday**.
g I've done a lot of silly things in **2017** / **a few moments ago** / **over the years**.

Change the sentences so they are true for you.

Vocabulary

1 **Who do these things belong to? Label the pictures with the words in the box.**

au pair	butcher	DJ
engineer	farmer	flight attendant
~~pilot~~	soldier	surgeon

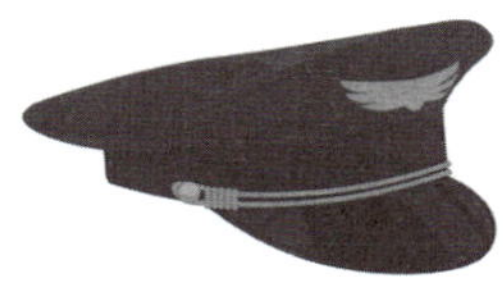

a __pilot__

f ___________

b ___________

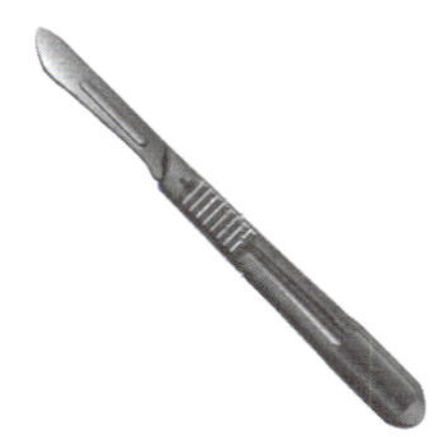

g ___________

c ___________

h ___________

d ___________

i ___________

e ___________

2 **Match the job in the box with the texts (a–g).**

~~actor~~	archaeologist	CEO
cook	telesales person	tour guide
vet		

a I've been in a few movies, but I like being on stage in a theater best. Last year, I was in "Hamlet" and I got excellent reviews. ___actor___

b At first, this was just a summer job, but I really enjoyed it. I love reading history books and I like showing people the interesting parts of my town. ________

c I have a marketing company and we now have about ninety employees. I think I know the names of all my staff. ________

d I spend most of my time with farmers and I work outdoors a lot. But in the village, people come to see me with their dogs and cats when they are sick. ________

e I studied it at college, of course, but I was lucky to get the job. I work for a museum in Mexico City and we are studying Aztec ruins in this part of the country. ________

f I work in a large factory and I run the kitchens there. We have to prepare meals for about four hundred people and I'm responsible for buying all the food. ________

g I work in a large office. It's very noisy because we are all talking on the phone all the time. We sell photocopiers and other office machines. ________

3 **Complete the sentences with the phrases in the box.**

a break	~~a day~~	a decision
a living	money	a part-time job
permission	two weeks	

a I'm going to have ___a day___ off tomorrow and go for a long walk.

b I asked my boss for ________ to leave work early.

c I need to make ________ about my future.

d I think I'll take ________ now and finish the work later.

e I usually have ________ off in the summer and go on vacation with my family.

f I'd like to make ________ as a model.

g I'm hoping to find ________ in the evenings and on the weekends.

h The job isn't well-paid and I don't make much ________.

4 **Complete the sentences with an appropriate verb.**

a It's extremely difficult to ___find___ a well-paid job.

b Every morning, they ________ a fifteen-minute coffee-break.

c He only wanted to ________ a nap, but he slept for three hours.

d In some countries, men can ________ some time off when their wife has a baby.

e Is it really possible to ________ a living as a snowboarder?

f The factory is closing and she's going to ________ her job.

g Why don't you ________ your parents for their advice?

h You can ________ a lot of money as a sales person, but you have to be good.

5 **Match the sentence beginnings (a–g) with their endings (1–7).**

a Women live longer than men, so they should

b People who do stressful jobs should

c Before they are allowed to run a country, politicians should

d The CEOs of large corporations that lose money should

e Employees who are often late shouldn't

f People in important jobs, like nurses and police officers, shouldn't

g Pilots and drivers who are responsible for people's lives shouldn't

1 be allowed to have vacations.

2 continue working after the age of 55.

3 earn less than pop stars or DJs.

4 get longer paid vacations than other people.

5 learn how to run a business.

6 resign immediately.

7 retire when they're older.

a	b	c	d	e	f	g
7						

Check (✓) the statements that you agree with.

Pronunciation

20 **Listen to the recording and read the text. Notice the pauses and how some words are linked together. Then practice reading it while you listen to the recording.**

Hi! / /

My name's Carlos, / / and‿I come from / Formosa / in Argentina. / /

I work‿as‿an‿artist / for‿an‿advertising company, / / but I‿also teach‿English. / /

I've been with‿the company / for‿a couple‿of years / / and‿I‿enjoy my work. / /

Listening

1 21 Cover the listening script and listen to two people playing a game. One person thinks of a job and the other person has to guess what it is. Check (✓) the two jobs that they describe.

a a dishwasher

d a lifeguard

b a waiter

e a flight attendant

c a cook

f a pilot

2 Listen again and number the questions in the order in which they're mentioned.

- [ ] Do you have to be strong?
- [ ] Do you have to wear a uniform?
- [ ] Do you need any training for this job?
- [1] Do men do this job?
- [ ] Do you travel a lot in this job?
- [ ] Do you work indoors?
- [ ] Do you work normal office hours?

3 Answer the questions in Exercise 2.

	Game 1	Game 2
1	Yes	
2		
3		
4		
5		
6		
7		

Ann:	So, do men do this job?
Bob:	Er, yes, men. And women.
Ann:	OK, do you work indoors or outdoors?
Bob:	I can only say "yes" or "no."
Ann:	OK, do you work indoors?
Bob:	Yes.
Ann:	Do you use your hands in this job?
Bob:	Yes.
Ann:	Do you need any training for this job?
Bob:	Yes. Usually.
Ann:	Do you work normal office hours?
Bob:	No.
Ann:	Do you have to work in the evenings?
Bob:	Yes.
Ann:	Do you have to be strong?
Bob:	No, not really.
Ann:	Do you travel a lot?
Bob:	No. Not at all.
Ann:	Is it a hot and smelly job?
Bob:	Er, yes, I suppose so.
Ann:	I think I've got it. Do you work in a restaurant?
Bob:	Yes.
Ann:	I know. You're a waiter?
Bob:	No!
Ann:	OK, so you're a cook?
Bob:	Yes, that's right. OK, my turn. Is it a job for men or women? I mean, do men usually do this job?
Ann:	Yes, men, usually. But women do it, too.
Bob:	Do you work indoors?
Ann:	Mm, well, no ... but I don't work outdoors!
Bob:	Is it a stressful job?
Ann:	Yes, sometimes. Sometimes very stressful.
Bob:	Do you need any training for this job?
Ann:	Yes. A lot.
Bob:	Do you work in an office?
Ann:	No.
Bob:	Do you earn a decent salary?
Ann:	Yes, I'm really well paid.
Bob:	Do you have to wear a uniform?
Ann:	Yes.
Bob:	Do you have to be strong?
Ann:	No! Not at all.
Bob:	Oh, er, I don't know. Do you travel a lot in this job?
Ann:	Yes. A lot.
Bob:	Ah, I've got it! You're a flight attendant! Oh, no, that's not possible. A lot of women do that job. I know – you're a pilot.
Ann:	Yes, at last.

Notes

Notes

Notes

Notes

Notes